Backyard Animals
Mountain Goats

Laura Pratt

www.av2books.com

AV[2] provides enriched content that supplements and complements this book. Weigl's AV[2] books strive to create inspired learning and engage young minds in a total learning experience.

Your AV[2] Media Enhanced books come alive with...

Audio
Listen to sections of the book read aloud.

Key Words
Study vocabulary, and complete a matching word activity.

Video
Watch informative video clips.

Quizzes
Test your knowledge.

Embedded Weblinks
Gain additional information for research.

Slide Show
View images and captions, and prepare a presentation.

Go to www.av2books.com, and enter this book's unique code.

Try This!
Complete activities and hands-on experiments.

BOOK CODE

F580990

AV[2] by Weigl brings you media enhanced books that support active learning.

... and much, much more!

Published by AV[2] by Weigl
350 5th Avenue, 59th Floor
New York, NY 10118
Website: www.av2books.com   www.weigl.com

Library of Congress Cataloging-in-Publication Data

Pratt, Laura.
 Mountain goats / Laura Pratt.
    p. cm. -- (Backyard animals)
 Includes index.
 ISBN 978-1-61690-623-8 (hardcover : alk. paper) -- ISBN 978-1-61690-629-0 (softcover : alk. paper)
 1. Mountain goat--Juvenile literature. I. Title.

 QL737.U53P73 2011
 599.64′75--dc22

                                    2010045192

Printed in the United States of America in North Mankato, Minnesota
1 2 3 4 5 6 7 8 9 0 15 14 13 12 11

052011
WEP37500

Editor Aaron Carr   **Design** Terry Paulhus

Every reasonable effort has been made to trace ownership and to obtain permission to reprint copyright material. The publishers would be pleased to have any errors or omissions brought to their attention so that they may be corrected in subsequent printings.

Photo Credits
Weigl acknowledges Getty Images as its primary photo supplier for this title.

Contents

Meet the Mountain Goat

Mountain goats are **mammals** that live on high, steep mountain slopes in parts of North America. They can often be seen resting on rocky cliffs that **predators** cannot reach.

Mountain goats are excellent climbers. They can grip rough, slippery surfaces without falling. This is because mountain goats have **cloven** hoofs. The hoofs can spread wide to help mountain goats keep their balance. Rubbery pads on the hoofs keep mountain goats from slipping.

Mountain goats have narrow heads with thin, black horns. They have thick, white fur that protects them from temperatures as low as –50˚ Fahrenheit (–46˚ Celsius).

Mountain goats can jump distances of about 12 feet (3.5 meters).

Mountain goats have a claw on the back of each leg. These claws act like brakes, helping the goat go downhill at an even speed.

All about Mountain Goats

Female mountain goats are called nannies, and males are called billies. Baby mountain goats are called kids. Nannies spend much of the year in a **herd** with their kids. Billies either live alone or with one or two other billies.

Mountain goats are found high in the Rocky and Cascade Mountains of North America. They live mostly above the **tree line**. Mountain goats make their homes in some of the world's most dangerous landscapes. They are the largest mammals that live at very high **altitudes**.

Mountain goats often live as high as 1.9 miles (3 kilometers) above sea level.

Male and Female Mountain Goats

Billy Goat	Nanny Goat
• Weighs up to 300 pounds (136 kilograms) • Thick horns that bend backward in a smooth curve	• Weighs 130 to 200 pounds (60 to 90 kg) • Thin horns that are usually straight at the base and curved near the end

Mountain Goat History

Scientists believe **ancestors** of the mountain goat arrived in North America about 100,000 years ago. These goats likely came from Asia to Alaska. Then, they started to move south.

Fossils of mountain goats have been found in the southern United States. Mountain goats lived in these southern areas during the **Ice Age**. When the frozen ground began to thaw, mountain goats moved north. Today, they are mostly found in western Canada and Alaska.

Fascinating Facts

Explorer Alexander Henry recorded the first sighting of a mountain goat in North America in 1811.

The mountain goat's white fur has led scientists to believe that the animal has always lived in snowy places.

Mountain Goat Shelter

Mountain goats live in the mountains year round. They rest on steep cliff faces and stay in areas where there is not much snow on the ground.

Most of the year, mountain goats stay high in the mountains. They **migrate** to lower areas during winter. However, even in the winter, mountain goats usually remain above the tree line.

Mountain goats are not suited to traveling long distances. They tire quickly when running and climbing over challenging mountain slopes. Instead, mountain goats tend to stay in small areas where they eat all of the plants they can find. When they have eaten the plants in one area, the mountain goats move to another area.

Mountain goats can climb slopes as steep as 60 degrees.

Nannies stand below their kids on mountain ledges. This allows them to stop a fall if their kid loses its balance.

Mountain Goat Features

Mountain goats spend most of their lives in areas where the weather can be extremely cold. For this reason, their bodies have **adapted** to life in these harsh conditions. Mountain goats have physical features that are well suited to the icy, windy climates in which they live.

COAT

A mountain goat's woolly white coat acts as **camouflage** during the winter. The coat is made of an underlayer of fine, dense wool and an overlayer of longer, hollow hairs that protect the mountain goat from snow and water. In the summer, mountain goats rub against rocks and trees to shed some of this thick coat.

LEGS

Mountain goats have short, strong legs to help them move through their mountain environment.

HORNS

A mountain goat's horns are between 2 and 10 inches (5 and 25 centimeters) long. The horns keep growing throughout the life of the mountain goat. Mountain goats use their horns for fighting. However, mountain goats do not fight often.

EYES

Mountain goats have excellent eyesight. They can see a moving object one mile (1.6 km) away.

BEARD

Both male and female mountain goats have beards that keep their face warm. The beards are part of their **mane**. A mountain goat's beard grows longer and fuller with age.

What Do Mountain Goats Eat?

Mountain goats are herbivores. This means they only eat plants. Mountain goats **graze** on the grasses, flowers, hemlock, trees, berries, and shrubs that grow in the mountains. They will eat almost any plant they can find.

Mountain goats are ruminants. This means they chew and swallow everything twice. After chewing and swallowing the first time, mountain goats will bring this food back up and chew it again. The food brought back up is called cud.

Mountain goats spend so much time eating that they often grind their teeth down to the gums.

Mountain goats move to higher ground in the summer. More plants grow in the area at that time of year.

Mountain Goat Life Cycle

Nannies and billies mate in the fall. Nannies give birth to one kid every spring. On rare occasions, a nanny will give birth to two kids.

Birth

At birth, mountain goats normally weigh about 7 pounds (3 kg). Kids are able to stand and eat a few minutes after birth. Within a couple of hours, kids start to run and climb.

One Day to One Month

After three days, a kid's horns start to show on its head. By three weeks, kids weigh about 40 pounds (18 kg). Kids drink their mother's milk for the first six weeks.

Almost half of all mountain goats die in their first year of life. This is most often because of **avalanches**, rock slides, and severe weather. Those that survive their first year usually live for about 12 years.

One Month to One Year

Kids stay close to their mother for the first year of life. The nannies and kids stay together in groups of up to 20.

Adult

Mountain goats are considered adults at about three years of age. As adults, nannies and billies live apart from one another. Males and females gather every fall for mating season.

Encountering Mountain Goats

Meeting a mountain goat in the wild is unlikely. This is because they live in places that are difficult to reach.

In winter, mountain goats sometimes come down to roads that run through mountains. They gather on and around highways to lick the salt people have put down to melt ice on the road. People driving mountain highways during winter months should watch for mountain goats and other animals.

If people do encounter mountain goats in the wild, it is recommended to keep a safe distance away from them. Mountain goats are not aggressive, but they can charge if they feel threatened.

Fascinating Facts

Mountain goats do not usually butt heads. Instead, they use their horns to poke each other in the back end.

Females are the leaders in mountain goat herds. Nannies often claim the best feeding grounds for their herd and force the males to leave.

Myths and Legends

Mountain goats appear in the myths and legends of many peoples around the world. They appear most often in the legends of the Aboriginal Peoples of North America. In these stories, mountain goats are often a symbol of strength and **agility**.

A group of Canadian Aboriginal Peoples call themselves "The Mountain Goat People." Like mountain goats, these people live on a mountain. For them, the right to hunt mountain goats is an honor. Only certain families are allowed to hunt mountain goats.

Many Aboriginal Peoples use mountain goat fur and fleece to make clothing.

The Great Race

The Sinixt Aboriginal Peoples tell a tale about how mountain goats and eagles came to live together in the mountains.

Long ago, a race was held to find out who was the best runner in the land. The prize for winning the race was a beautiful eagle. A group of mountain goats came down from the mountains to run in the race. However, the mountain goats were not welcomed when they arrived. The people did not like the mountain goats.

The people did not think the mountain goats could win. They decided to let the mountain goats run in the race. During the race, the mountain goats came to a cliff. They ran across the steep rock. None of the other runners could do this. The mountain goats won the race.

After the race, the mountain goats walked back to their mountain. The eagle followed and stayed with the mountain goats for the rest of her life. Today, eagles still build their nests in mountains.

Frequently Asked Questions

Are mountain goats actually goats?

Answer: Mountain goats are not true goats, but they are close relatives. They are properly known as goat-antelopes. Part of the scientific name for a mountain goat is *Oreamnos*. This name comes from Greek words that mean "mountain lamb."

How can someone tell the age of a mountain goat?

Answer: Mountain goats reveal their age through the number of rings on their horns. A new ring is added each year. If it has been a good year for food, the ring will be thick. If it has not, the ring will be thin.

How agile are mountain goats on tough terrain?

Answer: Mountain goats are well known for their speed and agility on steep mountain slopes. In 20 minutes, they can climb more than 1,476 feet (450 m).

Words to Know

adapted: adjusted to the natural environment

agility: the ability to move quickly and gracefully

altitude: the height of something from sea level

ancestors: relatives from the past

avalanches: sudden rushes of snow and ice down a mountain slope

camouflage: to use color to blend into an environment

cloven: animals with hoofs that are split into two toes

fossils: traces of an animal that are left behind in rocks

graze: to feed on growing grass

herd: a group of animals

Ice Age: a time when most of Earth was covered with ice

mammals: animals that have warm blood and feed milk to their young

mane: the long hair along the top and sides of the neck of certain mammals

migrate: to move from one area to another

predators: animals that hunt other animals for food

tree line: the altitude above sea level beyond which trees no longer grow

Index

Log on to www.av2books.com

AV² by Weigl brings you media enhanced books that support active learning. Go to www.av2books.com, and enter the special code found on page 2 of this book. You will gain access to enriched and enhanced content that supplements and complements this book. Content includes video, audio, web links, quizzes, a slide show, and activities.

Audio
Listen to sections of the book read aloud.

Video
Watch informative video clips.

Embedded Weblinks
Gain additional information for research.

Try This!
Complete activities and hands-on experiments.

WHAT'S ONLINE?

Try This!	Embedded Weblinks	Video	EXTRA FEATURES
Identify different types of mountain goats.	Find out more information on mountain goat identification.	Watch a video about mountain goat behavior.	**Audio** Listen to sections of the book read aloud.
List important features of the mountain goat.	Learn more about the history of mountain goats.	See a mountain goat in its natural environment.	**Key Words** Study vocabulary, and complete a matching word activity.
Compare the similarities and differences between young and adult mountain goats.	Complete an interactive activity.		**Slide Show** View images and captions, and prepare a presentation.
Test your knowledge of mountain goats.	Learn more about what to do when encountering mountain goats.		**Quizzes** Test your knowledge.
	Read more mountain goat stories and legends.		

AV² was built to bridge the gap between print and digital. We encourage you to tell us what you like and what you want to see in the future.

Sign up to be an AV² Ambassador at www.av2books.com/ambassador.